EDOUARD BALLADUR

For a Union
of the West

between Europe
and the United States

T0167805

ABOUT THE AUTHOR

Edouard Balladur, prime minister of France in the early 1990s, brought about extensive market reforms as minister of the economy in the 1980s. Author of a number of books, he is an independent thinker as well as a political figure. He has been a leader within the Gaullist movement for many decades, and is credited with having drawn the mainstream French Gaullists back into a pro–European Union stance and into abandoning anti-American attitudes. He has often been called the mentor of Nicolas Sarkozy, now President of France: Sarkozy rose within Balladur's wing of the Gaullist movement and was once spokesman for Balladur. The *International Herald Tribune* wrote that Balladur's book constitutes the "underlying premise" of Sarkozy's policies.

EDOUARD BALLADUR

For a Union
of the West
between Europe
and the United States

HOOVER INSTITUTION PRESS

Stanford University   Stanford, California

Hoover Institution Press Publication No. 566
Copyright © 2009 by the Board of Trustees of the
Leland Stanford Junior University

First printing, American edition, 2009
Manufactured in the United States of America
15 14 13 12 11 10 09   9 8 7 6 5 4 3 2
The paper used in this publication meets the minimum requirements of the American National Standard for Information Sciences Permanence of Paper for Printed Library Materials, ANSI Z39.48–1992. ♾

Library of Congress Cataloging-in-Publication Data

Balladur, Edouard, 1929–
[Pour une union occidentale entre l'Europe et les Etats-Unis. English]
For a union of the West between Europe and the United States / by Edouard Balladur.
    p.   cm.— (Hoover Institution Press publication ; no. 566)
ISBN-13: 978-0-8179-4932-7 (pbk. : alk. paper)
1. Western countries—Foreign relations. 2. Europe—Foreign relations—United States. 3. United States—Foreign relations—Europe. I. Title.
D863.B3513   2009
327.09182′1—dc22   2008039406

Original French edition, *Pour une Union occidentale entre l'Europe et les Etats-Unis*, (ISBN-13: 978–2–213–63421–0) was published by Fayard: ©Librairie Arthème Fayard, 2007.

This American edition is published with the cooperation and permission of the author and Librairie Arthème Fayard.

Translation by Jessica Abreu and Ira Straus, with Tiziana Stella, Ani Gevorkian, and Laura Gerhardt of the Streit Council for a Union of Democracies.

The Streit Council is a non-profit organization that works toward better-organized cooperation between the U.S. and Europe, along with the other OECD democracies. Based in Washington, D.C., it provides a non-partisan forum for policymakers and scholars to explore evolving inter-democracy relations, through conferences, scholarships, and reports on the functioning and future of inter-democracy institutions and their role in the global system. www.streitcouncil.org

Publication in the United States was made possible by the support of Howard H. Leach, former U.S. Ambassador to France, 2001–2005.

Contents

Introduction: Countering the Clash of Civilizations

D o we still have the right to speak of the West? When we do, are we fanning the flames, rekindling the hatreds, unleashing violence among peoples of different cultures and religions? Some would have you think so. Nothing could be further from the truth. Could anything be more important than self-reflection, than knowing what you hold most dear and who you are, so that you can build relationships with others based on realities and the truth and not merely on rehashing prefabricated ideas? To define oneself is not to hate what is different.

The West is a civilization inspired at one and the same time by classical thought and Christian faith, marked first by the progressive separation between religion and political power, then by the advent of democracy and the rule of law. It is characterized by the conviction that all men are equal, by its respect for freedom, its reverence for

1

independence and its mistrust of overly restrictive and imperious collectivities, which are suspected of wanting to impose their domination at all costs. Western civilization has long represented humanism and freedom in the eyes of the rest of the world. This is the face it has worn as it has emerged from history.

Defined in this way, the West consists essentially of Europe and North America (the United States and Canada). However, it has always aspired to spread its message of civilization beyond this geographical space and, assured of its unparalleled value, to set an example for others.

The great discoveries, the intellectual, scientific, and industrial revolutions, the conquest of colonial empires: for centuries, the West has dominated the world. By eliminating barriers, developing exchanges, and making continents communicate, Western Europe, then the United States, as rivals and partners, have extended their influence, set themselves up as models, the authors of international rule and masters of its sanction.

Today the West is divided and at the same time facing competition. It is proving incapable of organizing itself to face this ordeal, while its power and influence are under attack in every area. History is beginning to be made without the West; perhaps one day it will be made against it. There is only one way to avoid this: Westerners must become aware of the risk and realize that a greater solidarity among them is the only way to ward it off. They would hardly merit credit for doing so, as their interdependence leaps to the eyes of anyone willing to see things as they are. And they would still have to face up to the consequences, in the policies implemented on both sides of the Atlantic, by strengthening their ties, and joining together for common action in the world.

༃

For those willing to face it, the reality is simple: In a world riven by ethnic and religious conflicts, and the threats of radical Islamism, terrorism, and international crime, the dissipation of the West's strengths, parceled out among states whose influence is being slowly eroded by natural evolution, is harmful. The emergence of the countries of Asia, Latin America, even Africa, will each day further deprive the West of its supremacy. It must organize itself to defend its principles, its convictions and its civilization; it is a matter of political and moral duty. The United

States cannot expect to decide everything on its own; its failure in the disastrous war it took on in Iraq is proof of this. It needs a strong ally. This ally can only be the European Union, on whose soil the modern world was born. Failing this, the West will have great difficulty in awakening to what unites it and in ensuring its survival.

Without France, Europe will not attain the position and status of political actor on the world stage; on France's choice depends the future of the European Union. France must make its contribution to this work of understanding and concord. One can notice two tendencies in this regard.

First, those who are tempted by pessimism, with a tinge of declinism. France is perceived as disengaging on the economic front, as being excessively attached to the status quo, and to the acquired rights of each social class. It is seen as no longer being in a position to influence the course of events or master its own destiny; a middling power, it shrinks from its obligation to reform in order to survive and holds onto fantasies drawn from a glorious past and kept alive by sterile nostalgia.

In the second camp are the romantics. In the name of the will of France, glorified to the point of risking isolation before the rest of the world, they cultivate a lyrical, even grandiloquent style, an ambition that is out of proportion to its means, a systematic and irrational anti-Americanism in which they see the mark of patriotism and independence, a self-satisfaction tainted by arrogance, a blindness to reality.

Neither of these attitudes is justified. France must act, not give in to pessimism or cultivate boastfulness. It holds one of the keys to the world of tomorrow. Despite the doubts that plague it, in the eyes of the rest of the world it still counts; let it reason coldly, banish the narrowly jingoistic spirit, and act on the facts as they are. It can take the initiative and propose a new alliance between Europe and America, further still: a true union.

This is the challenge before our country in the coming decades.

৵

Further: We will have to abandon our illusions, kept alive at great expense, and show signs of realism, even while avoiding vague debates that give rise to an abundance of great questions to which there are no answers, and to pompous but ineffectual assertions. True ambition is incompatible with pipe dreams. If we want our civilization to survive, we must confront the dangers we know only too well.

From continent to continent, barriers are being lowered, borders are being crossed, men come and go everywhere, are informed of everything, everything is known, repeated, almost everything is seen. The world is becoming more uniform, but it is also becoming increasingly dangerous as it falls victim to nuclear proliferation, climate problems, population imbalances, trade competition, and inequalities in the distribution of wealth and knowledge. The passions are still there, raging, kept alive by the rivalries of history and by today's conflicts of interest.

What remedy can there be to the violence smoldering here and there that the smallest spark could set ablaze? The creation of a true international community, capable of enacting rules and enforcing them universally, collides with the sovereignty of states; in fact, some advocate a return to the exercise of full powers by nation-states, which are seen as the only bodies entitled to true existence and legitimacy, with no thought given to the regression and disorder that would result. Multilateralism is also mentioned as allowing a happy equilibrium among the various axes of power constituted by the United States, Europe,

Russia, China, India, and Brazil; but who can fail to see that such an equilibrium can only flow from reciprocal goodwill, the existence of which is barely perceptible? The United States, dominant for so long, is confronted with continent-sized countries that appear or reappear on the world stage and whose openness to concessions is waning in proportion to the increase of their power. As for the European Union, it has, for half a century now, demonstrated its ability to create economic progress, even to spread democracy to the East, but also its inability to arouse among its partners a modicum of fear, and thereby respect.

Today the world seems to be slipping away from the Western powers. Their material strength remains unparalleled, but their moral strength and self-confidence are continuing to weaken. They are not able to answer clearly the questions they are confronted with: Should they now seek to maintain the old style of domination at all costs? Is this still possible? Is it even desirable? We know what the result of it would be. Should they, to the contrary, take note of the fact that the West is no longer the sole dominant power in a more balanced world, one where its will alone no longer determines the law? That would be more realistic, more reasonable. But if they accept this reality, they must not abandon their principles or their long term interests.

～

It is high time for Europe and America to awaken to all that unites them in their traditions, their cultures, their ideals, to that which draws them together, be it on the economic, moral, political, or strategic level. They are the most threatened by the chaos in the world and the emergence of new powers that do not adhere to the same principles as they do, whose conceptions of life, man, and society are different. A true union between Europe and the United States must be devised. It is not a matter of joining forces against the rest of the world, but rather of ensuring the survival of the civilization that they brought to the world and that they are responsible for passing on to future generations.

Let us beware of the facile use of language! To put a label of "occidentalism" on a new ambition of the West and treat it as equivalent to radical Islamism: this is surely nonsensical. To our knowledge, the West advocates neither the enforcement of religious law for all, nor the denial of individual freedoms, nor the use of violence as a weapon of political debate. It has at times betrayed its principles—no one is immune to the temptations of power and selfishness, the colonial period demonstrated this—but at least it had them.

To come to terms with the original vocation of the West, with its historical right to defend its character and its interests, is not to encourage the dreaded clash of civilizations; to the contrary, it is to contribute to a new equilibrium in an unstable world, one that is evolving very fast, where the affirmation by each people of its character must be accompanied by solidarity among them all. No civilization will win out over any other, that time has passed; all must agree to dialogue, cooperation, and preserving their differences without exacerbating them to the point of confrontation.

The clash of civilizations will not be avoided by weakening a particular civilization. This is especially true of the civilization of which we are the heirs and the guardians. It deserves, as do others to which the greatest part of humanity belongs, to be respected and preserved. It is not a matter of vouching for narrow-minded selfishness or proclaiming superiority of any sort. Rather it is a matter of affirming our faith in the permanence of an age-old civilization.

I

❧

EUROPE AND AMERICA HAVE STRAINED RELATIONS

Five centuries ago, the intellectual renaissance and the scientific revolution gave Europe the empire of the world. It extended its dominion every which way, colonized countries with ancient civilizations, harnessed new lands, put its men at the controls, and imposed its techniques and its way of thinking. The entire world breathed at the pace set by England, France, the Netherlands and Spain. The United States, formed first by peoples from Northern Europe who had resisted the divine right of kings, won its freedom from English domination and, having conquered an enormous country that extended from the Atlantic to the Pacific, became the most powerful nation in the world. Europe, twice torn asunder by continent-wide civil wars, thought it was the only theater on the planet where the fate of power would be played out. It was punished by its blind self-centeredness and fell into dependence on the United States, which had liberated it from Nazi occupation and protected it against the Soviet threat of extending its hold in the East. Then it got back on its feet, with the help of the United States, and dreamed of leveling the playing field by unifying and thus balancing its influence; to date, it has not succeeded. The United States is politically closer to the European countries than any others, but does not show them any particular regard, save for a certain attention to appearances, and even this with difficulty.

The world is becoming unified technically, economically, and commercially, somewhat less so culturally; new powers are emerging and reviving a sometimes-glorious past; on the power scales, the relative weight of Europe and the United States is shrinking. Even worse: they are the objects of a growing hostility from the rest of the world, which hasn't forgotten that the West colonized, dominated, raped, and exploited it, that it sought to impose its principles, its rules for collective life, its ideals, and to dispossess others of their cultures, ways of life and traditional religions. To no avail, it must be said; all that the West gained was the arousal of distrust and animosity. History is taking its revenge.

༄

Immersed in these troubles, Europe and America have yet to understand that, for the most part, the dangers that threaten them are the same. They must present a united front.

Conflicts in Africa, in Asia, between countries that are unsure of themselves and whose borders are contested, instability in Latin America, up-heavals in the balance of power in the Asia-Pacific region and the Near East, weakness of the UN, constant violations of the very foundations of international law, which could have been as-sumed to be accepted by all, economic instability, monetary chaos, trade rivalries rooted in the de-velopment of emancipated nations, fears of en-ergy shortages and pandemics, environmental destruction, massive movements of populations fleeing poverty towards countries where they hope to find a better life, multiplication of ethnic and religious conflicts, intolerance and rejection of differences, the arms race, the temptation to turn inward, fear of the future. . . . The entire structure built in 1945 on the ruins of world conflict is crumbling and everything needs to be re-thought.

No simple or obvious answers exist to such serious questions. Certainly neither Europe nor America alone possesses them. But each needs to talk to the other, because both are vitally concerned by the worsening situation in a world that has become more prosperous, yet more imbalanced. Too often they confront one another during international meetings, to no great avail for either. Short-term selfishness gains the upper hand and they have great difficulty in coming to any agreement, when it is their common fate that is at stake: the preservation of their influence and the destiny of their power. Their relations are marred by incomprehension, misunderstandings, and mutual resentments. Europe and the United States talk to one another a great deal, but most often it is to discover their disagreements and attempt in vain to resolve them.

～

It is true that there are many differences between them—demographically, politically, economically, militarily, diplomatically. The United States ranks first in the world as a destination for immigrants: close to eight million people have settled there, legally or illegally, in the past four years. The annual rate is three times higher than during the great wave of Europeans who arrived in the New World around 1910. The birthrate in America is higher and more dynamic than in other wealthy countries. With three hundred million people, the United States ranks third among the most populated countries of the world behind China and India. In 2005, its ethnic composition reflected a growing diversity: next to its majority population of European origin, there are more than forty million inhabitants of Latin American origin, another forty million of African origin, fifteen million of Asian origin, and five million Native Americans and native Alaskans.

As for the European Union, it has close to five hundred million people; its most highly populated country is Germany at eighty-two million. The birthrate is lower than in the United States, the mortality rate higher, the balance of migration lower, and the fertility rate much lower. All of this means a more fragile demographic structure, with a gloomier future. And it does nothing to heighten any respect that Americans might have for a Europe with declining demographics and—they are convinced of it—a vacillating will.

The political differences are no less striking.

There is an American nationalism allied to a messianic ideology, joining the tradition of Theodore Roosevelt with that of Wilson. This is the new American ideology. Meanwhile Europe, which knows that it has little control over events, rejects power politics and is content with an ill-defined multilateralism for its justification. This comes as no surprise, given that it has neither the military means of power nor the will to acquire them. In the affairs of the world there is an American will, which while questionable at times, is clearly stated. There is no clear and strong European will. The European Union appears weak on the military and diplomatic fronts, dependent upon the initiatives of others, struggling to put instead before them any sound and credible proposals of its own. It seems to have little desire to play a role of its own, preferring to limit itself to financial and economic assistance to countries in crisis; its contribution to military peacekeeping efforts is proportionately much lower.

Is this European attitude a sign of weakness, as suggested by Robert Kagan, with weakness being defined here as a preference for negotiation? Is it not rather the expression of a deep moral and ideological conviction? Ever since the first postwar period and the League of Nations, for which

Briand proselytized, could it not be that, for maintaining the peace, Europeans have believed exclusively in the construction of an international society founded on respect for law, whereas the United States, having left its isolationism behind, has relied above all on relations based on power?

America's view of its own power is such that it distorts its judgment; by contrast, the European Union struggles to assert itself, behaving as if it were lacking confidence and plagued by self-doubt. The Alliance, which is intended to unite them, is out of balance, so great is the assurance of the Americans and the resignation of the Europeans. When the heads of state of the twenty-seven members of the European Union meet with the President of the United States, you would think you had traveled back in time and were witnessing the Roman Emperor gathering around himself his vassal monarchs.

～

Imagine this situation: Europe and the United States are threatened by identical risks. They have common interests far stronger than those that divide them, shared convictions, a single civilization that should bind them as one, a shared vision of man's role, his place in society and the world, and economic means of equal size (even if not organized equally well for use). Everything should draw them closer together. Yet they continue to cling to quarrels of another time, as if the world had not changed, as if they were still in a position to contend alone for world domination.

Let them finally open their eyes! Whatever they might wish, each is deeply dependent upon the other. Europe has no better possible ally than America. America has no better possible ally than Europe. True, many doubt this on both sides of the Atlantic. But let them consider History, and the dangers both are faced with. Let them reflect before it is too late and before their divisions, cultivated with persistent care, have done irreparable damage.

II

ঌৎ

WILL THE WORLD BUILD A NEW EQUILIBRIUM WITHOUT THE WEST?

While it has not yet happened, the risk exists. The West faces competition, a situation without precedent for several centuries; bit by bit, this is eroding the position it holds and the influence it wields.

In demographic terms, the European Union is not the only power in crisis: both Russia and Japan are faced with the same predicament. But this is no consolation. Consider countries such as Germany, Spain or Italy: for several decades the average number of children per woman has barely exceeded one, and each age group loses a third to a fourth of its numbers compared to previous generations. Despite significant immigration, the population will decrease. Over the next ten years, Germany will lose ten to fifteen million inhabitants.

At the same time, the populations of Africa, Latin America and Asia, despite certain internal disparities, are increasing massively. A number of Third World countries are undergoing a population explosion, whose effects account by themselves for the entire growth in world population.

No doubt the United States is in a better situation to withstand this "demographic shock" than Europe. Nonetheless, the world's less developed regions will expand from just over five billion to nearly eight billion inhabitants by 2050, whereas the developed regions, mainly the West, will maintain a stable population of around one billion two hundred million. This stability will be thanks entirely to the immigration that the United States, which has not forgotten its origins, will welcome much more readily than Europe, where the deterrents to immigration are being multiplied, the better to control it. From this point of view, we undoubtedly have two Wests, one more open, the other more closed off. In any case, the decline in fertility and increase in longevity will lead to a rapid aging of the population, not only in the West, but also in a growing number of other countries, including China which practices rigorous birth control.

It is not just the demographic trend that is

playing out to the disadvantage of the West; it is also the competition among economies. The economies of the Asia-Pacific region are expanding at a rapid pace, nearly 10 percent a year, per capita as well as in total output; growth in the United States and Europe is far less dynamic. For many years, economic growth in developing countries and economies in transition has been stronger than that of the developed world. In this regard, Europe is at a greater disadvantage than the United States, but both are in a weakened position compared to the rest of the world.

A number of factors converge to sustain a high rate of economic growth in emerging countries: the progressive increase in investment, the export boom, infrastructure development, the steady rise in credit, and growth in domestic demand. From now on, the dynamism of the world will be coming from these countries. They are accumulating colossal trade surpluses; China has, on this basis alone, amassed funds that are greatly expanding its reserves and allowing it not only to finance the deficits of more developed economies, primarily the United States, but also to develop its foreign investments. Who is more dependent on the other: the lender or the borrower? The experts debate this question with great erudition. If the situation is unhealthy for all concerned, it carries dangers particularly for those who consume a lot without producing or saving enough.

꒘

With this ongoing shift in energy and wealth, is it any surprise that a mentality of revenge should develop among emerging nations, giving rise to a clash of wills to power? This can be seen in the cultural sphere. The values of the West are being held up as an object for rejection; in all the media a discourse is developed that relativizes the principles of human rights, casts doubt on the benefits of individualism, and contests the rules of democracy. All of this happens with the complicity of the European countries, ever willing to accept tyrannies elsewhere and think of them as temporary, hoping thereby to preserve their interests and influence, or to fight better against the religious extremism that they would like to see as the only real danger. The cultural backlash has been spreading, not only in the Muslim world, but also throughout Asia and Africa. For those in power in these areas, the struggle for human rights seems more like a tactic of those who contest their authority than a sincere conviction.

The same will to power—or should we call it

a self-affirmation, a renaissance?—is apparent in the strategic and military arena. One need only consider China's policies in Africa and Pakistan, or the Strait of Malacca where for China it is a matter of securing its energy supply channels militarily.

This will to assert oneself, to count, to be respected, is also taking hold in those countries of the South that are attempting to put the West on the defensive by organizing coalitions against it, so as to marginalize it in international negotiations. It is in this way that Brazil, India, and South Africa, putting themselves forth as the three great developing democracies, recently decided to defend their common interests together on the international stage. According to the Brazilian president, this new alliance constitutes a public affirmation that the three countries' leaders believe in "South-South relations," and that in their view it is never too late to change the economic and commercial geography of the world.

Despite their sometimes divergent interests in agricultural or industrial affairs, and their great inequality in power, these three giants took up, on their respective continents, the challenge they had set for themselves, and strengthened "South-

South" cooperation. They demonstrated their solidarity in several international forums, together called for UN Security Council reform, opposed the agricultural exports barriers imposed by the wealthier nations, and demanded the resumption of the WTO negotiations. They furthermore developed or supported programs to fight hunger and poverty, and encouraged the exchange of medications for AIDS, tuberculosis and malaria.

And so it is that the solidarity among these nations, diplomatic and political at first, is now beginning to develop an economic component. These alliances are in their infancy but strengthening quickly, especially between India and Brazil. The three states seek to double trade among themselves from its 2007 level.

Europe and the United States are no longer the only ones making decisions and taking action. Other powers are emerging, creating new centers of prosperity and new trade flows. The equilibrium of the world is being shaken up; it is changing.

III

♒

THE WEST IS FACED WITH HOSTILITY FROM THE WORLD

If the risk exists that the world will work out its path of development without the West, catching it unawares and forcing it constantly to adapt, we have seen that a more serious problem exists: it is not only the marginalization of the West that is underway, but its rejection. How many of the countries of the world contest not only the West's material, economic and military domination, declining though it may be, but all of its moral values, and the principles that govern its collective life? This rejection can lead the West, and particularly the United States, to over-reactions, to systematic aggressiveness toward countries that question its predominance, the model it claims to represent, the Good it believes it embodies; thereby adding fuel to the fire of anti-Western resentment. A fateful example is the Iraqi disaster, the effects of which will be felt for a long time to come. The West must avoid giving in to a nearly paranoia mindset, feeling it is under attack from all sides, unjustly challenged, surrounded by enemies. It should instead compel itself to view things with a cool head, to understand what it really embodies in the eyes of others and the reasons for the hostility directed against it.

Kipling spoke of the mission of governing the planet as the "white man's burden." A burden continues to weigh on Western shoulders, but in a different sense. The exclusive mission the white man had attributed to himself now justifies his rejection by those who challenge him. The views of extremist organizations of all sorts, not just Islamist, bear witness to this trend, as do the views of a number of Third World leaders. The West's centuries of world domination are being succeeded by the century of resentment; the West is paying the price of its selfish and blind arrogance.

This rejection, nourished by a simplistic anti-Americanism that for many serves in place of a system of thought, exists even within the Western countries. One need only consider the anti-globalization movements and the French far left, for which globalization can by definition only be ultraliberal, and therefore reprehensible. McDonald's establishments are ransacked simply because it is an American company, without any further thought. Nor is the traditional French left immune from these Pavlovian reflexes. In their eyes, the smallest friendly gesture toward the United States can be stigmatized as revealing an "Atlanticist" position. In the context of these self-righteous knee-jerk reactions, praise for independence of spirit can be bestowed upon anyone who gives in to the most absurd simple-mindedness: European leaders can be seen visiting China and there criticizing the United States in the name of freedom!

Naturally, these excesses in turn call forth others that make the clash explicit and increase the risks of conflict. There is a temptation to escalation, and to overreactions in the West, especially in the United States; it feels itself an undeserving victim of the hostility, and is inclined to respond by affirming its power vis-à-vis those who reject it. We have witnessed such reactions for several decades now, in Asia as in Africa or Latin America. The West is aware of its relative weakening vis-à-vis competitors who now feel better positioned to present a challenge. It knows its own position is threatened; it wishes to preserve it; it reaffirms its leadership role, which it still thinks of as something invested in it by History. So the West resorts to traditional means of military and economic threat, but to no great avail. No one knows any longer how to resolve the problems of a world where the multiplication of the poles of power has reached the point of chaos. Indeed, how does one extricate oneself from the Iraqi quagmire, how does one deal with Iran and avoid nuclear proliferation, how does one answer international terrorism? No one knows.

༄

Faced with competition over its power and values, fearing marginalization, not to say rejection, and dreading the threat of violent actions provoked by terrorist states or international criminal organizations, the West must rise to the challenge. What new message should it deliver to the world? How should it organize itself? The West is hesitating, because it has still not become fully aware of its profound unity. Yet, if Europe and the United States do not share the same interests everywhere, and if they do not face the same threats in all cases, the fact remains that, in what is most important, they are in the same boat.

The Middle East's instability affects both sides of the Atlantic; for generations it has been a constant concern for both. None of their interventions has managed to create mutual recognition and peace among its peoples. It is their greatest common failure. Europe is geographically closer to this region, but the United States, with its military presence in Lebanon, Israel, Iraq and Turkey, plays a major role. Both depend on this region for energy; both are particularly vulnerable to terrorism.

Russia, for a decade after the collapse of the Soviet Union, seemed to be a stalled strategic competitor. This is no longer the case. This enormous country is on the verge of regaining its prosperity. It has put an end to the chaos that followed the downfall of communism. Even with a truncated territory and population, it is strengthening its ties to former vassals, which in many cases are having difficulty managing their emancipation. With its proximity to areas of conflict in Central Asia, its border with China with which it both colludes and competes, its concerns about growing American influence in the former Soviet republics and the geographical expansion of the Atlantic Alliance; with the second largest nuclear arsenal of the world, its permanent membership on the Security Council, its presence in the Pacific Ocean and its overtures to Japan when they serve its interests . . . Russia clearly intends to recover a large part of the role that it lost with the breakup of the Soviet Union. Russia is central to European concerns, as it borders numerous members of the European Union, and is the irreplaceable source of the energy that almost all members of the Union are lacking. To be sure, with its nostalgia for its former domination of Eastern Europe, Russia represents a greater risk for Europeans than for Americans, but it is determined, if not to compete with the latter for predominance, then at least to compel the United States to recognize it as a partner whose consent is indispensable in vital matters.

In Asia and the Pacific, the United States is more directly affected by risks rooted in the staggering economic growth of the developing countries: China's growing ambitions, the nationalist sentiments flourishing in Japan, and the unstable nature of relations among India, Pakistan, Afghanistan, and Iran. Recently America became aware that it has almost as much at stake as Europe in preventing Africa from sinking into misery and ethnic rivalry, in encouraging the continent to control its population growth, and in ensuring economic livelihood and health.

Even if differences of position and interest exist between the United States and Europe, with the former's growing orientation toward the Pacific and the latter's need to manage its own neighborhood in Africa, the Near East, and Central Asia, a basic solidarity remains between them. This solidarity is marked by the struggle for peace, for the defense of a specific political and moral civilization, and a struggle against poverty, nuclear proliferation and terrorism. Everything that weakens one weakens the other. Both Europe and the United States should become convinced of this reality and leave the games of the past behind them.

What could this solidarity achieve if the confrontation between the United States and China or the underlying tensions between Europe and Russia were to intensify? Is the West ready to form a common front against common threats or will it continue to act in an uncoordinated manner, when it acts at all? Will it finally admit that the shifting of the center of gravity of global power requires it to let go of its reflexive traditional thinking and ready-made ideas?

IV

⁂

DOES THE WEST HAVE AN UNDERLYING UNITY?

M any have their doubts. The differences between America and Europe are profound
and rooted in history. Culturally, writes Bruno
Tertrais*, the role of religion in public life separates America from Europe, as does the concept
of relations between church and state. Until September 11, 2001, America accepted expressions
of Muslim fundamentalism fairly willingly,
whereas a far more cautious attitude existed in
Europe, apart from Great Britain. No equivalent
exists in Europe to the rejection of Darwinism,
and American culture is less concerned about reg-

---

*Europe/Etats-Unis: valeurs communes ou divorce culturel?
(Europe/United States: Common Values or Cultural Divorce?), Note no. 36 of the Robert Schuman Foundation,
2006.

ulating the recourse to force, as if therein lies the natural God-given right of the strongest. Let us not forget the attitude toward the problems in the Near East, and the difficulty Europeans have in understanding the extent to which support for the Jewish state is anchored in American religious culture and its political mentality.

The forces that drive America are far different from those of Europe. America is young and remains a land of immigrants, and its very liberal economy is causing it to grow rapidly; Europe is aging, tends toward protectionism, and has great difficulty making reforms. It should come as no surprise that America's power and influence should be so much larger than Europe's on every level.

Nonetheless, the European Union, initially a product of the Cold War and the desire to guard against Soviet expansionist ambitions, has now come into its own as a great economic and monetary power that is willing to stand against the United States without hesitation. Furthermore, the end of the Cold War has made Europe safer, even if the fear of Russia that prevails in the former iron-curtain states is leading the United States to expand the Atlantic Alliance's field of action, thereby further linking the security of Europe and America.

The war led by the United States in Iraq has exacerbated its differences with Europe. These are no longer simply matters of material or political interest. A veritable ideological and moral rift now separates America from a number of European countries. To be sure, changes of leadership in Europe and the United States, combined with the evidence of the chaos that reigns in the Near East and the urgency of finding solutions and a way out, will someday ease the tensions. Nevertheless, a realization has occurred: On a question of vital importance for their futures, Europe and America are having difficulty coordinating their actions. This is a prospect equally frightening for both!

৵

And yet the West exists, hard as it is to define it. One could narrow the definition to the English-speaking world, but that would be inaccurate and dangerous, and would exclude Europe. To see it as the group of highly industrialized countries, all allies of the United States, would mean opening its doors to a number of Asian nations, overlooking historical traditions, and neglecting differences of culture and moral values. To try to organize a Eurasian security community "from Vancouver to Vladivostok" would mean bringing Russia into a group where, even if it accepted membership, both Russia and its partners would feel ill at ease.

The transatlantic community constitutes the best definition of the West. It is a material reality, grounded in facts. The economic integration between the two sides of the Atlantic is progressing continuously. Europe and America are each other's best clients and largest investors. The European Union is the preferred destination for American investments, and is in turn the primary investor in the United States. Over the past decade, American companies have invested ten times more in the Netherlands than in China, and Europe has invested more in Texas than the United States has in Japan.

Trade in goods has been growing at a rate of 10 percent a year, to the point that people now speak of a "transatlantic economy" embracing fifteen million jobs on the two sides of the ocean and transactions amounting to the equivalent of two billion euros every day. Together, the European Union and the United States still produce more than 55 percent of world GDP*, representing 24 percent of the world's exports, 31 percent of imports, and 62 percent of foreign direct investment. The North Atlantic will remain the commercial and financial center of the world for a long time to come.

The security of Europe and of America are closely linked, less by the risks left over from the Cold War than by those arising from terrorism, nuclear proliferation, and poorly managed globalization. The threat that weighs on them is largely the same; both are targets of choice for fundamentalist and terrorist movements that are horrified by their reverence for freedom. This imposes on them a need for common strategic choices, and the reinforcement of an alliance, formed after the World War to fend off the danger of Soviet domination in Europe, that retains its value in an unstable, militarily fragmented and uncertain world. In fact, the Atlantic Alliance is already extending its sphere of operations into Eastern Europe and Central Asia.

Europe and America harbor the same collec-

---

*The combined GDP of the European Union and United States was 58 percent of the world total, in nominal (ordinary) exchange rates, according to the IMF and World Bank statistics for 2006.

tive ideals, their history is largely shared, their principles likewise, and most of the American population is still of European origin. They both believe in democracy, and, while they put it into practice to varying degrees in different areas, they do so far more than the other parts of the world. They are deeply attached to fundamental human rights and individual liberty. They believe in the market economy, in competition, and in progress as the fruit of individual initiative. Above all, they are proud of having invented the concept of the rights of man, even if they don't always put these rights into practice in an exemplary fashion. This Euro-Atlantic space comprises nearly a billion people, divided among a multitude of nations with an eventful history; and despite ever-present rivalries, they are ultimately devoted to the same spiritual values.

Thus, not only are Europe and the United States bound together by the same fundamental interests, but, in addition, their societies rest on very similar ethical principles and face the same dangers. To unite the West, there is not only a powerful and active transatlantic economy, but also a deep community—a community of civilization and of the concept of freedom and collective life. What remains to be done is to breathe new life into this Western unity, which already is inscribed in history and in facts, and, no matter what some might claim, in our minds and mores. Whatever may be the differences between Europe and America—and various international proceedings supply the theater for them—the prosperity and peace of the world still depend largely on their cohesion. A political existence must be given to this Euro-American community.

ॐ

Will the European Union be capable one day of existing politically and pursuing independent policies, the indispensable condition for establishing more balanced and equal relations with the United States? If not, the West will remain a formula that serves as a front for the maintenance of American predominance. Despite the progress made since the war, this goal is still not in sight. It will only be attained if Europe manages to endow itself with the structure and powers that would enable it to be heard and have real weight. This will be no easy task.

The United States exercises considerable influence over Europe's economy and growth, and plays an essential role in ensuring the security of the continent. For a long time, American leaders saw the European Union as an extension of the Atlantic Alliance that they dominated. From the start, Washington's influence always tended in the same direction. It has sought to extend the geographical reach of the European Union, and avoid any strengthening of the Union's own powers within the Alliance, or within any of the other organizations for political or economic co-operation, the better to maintain its custody over the nations of the Old Continent. Seen from the other side of the Atlantic, a close correlation existed between European unification and the affirmation of American power, something further reinforced by globalization. Many in Washington were banking on a convergence between European supranational integration and American interests, as the European area would offer American companies a framework for activity no longer subject to border restrictions.

Those days are nearing their end. If the United States has long believed that rapprochement among European countries would favor the maintenance of its own influence in Europe, it is beginning to shed this illusion. Europe will increasingly be drawn to use its Union in order to give expression to an independent voice in world affairs, whether in debates at the United Nations or discussions at the World Trade Organization or the International Financial Institutions. More and more, industrial competition will rage among businesses on either side of the Atlantic. In the future, Europe's position will depend on what balance of forces it is able to achieve in relation to others. It remains for Europe to give itself the means.

☙

In a world that is so unified when one considers the material realities, yet so fragmented if one observes the movements of its hearts, the unity between Europe and America must win out over their differences. This assumes that America will accept that it is neither alone nor all-powerful, and that Europe will make the efforts needed to exist through something other than its grievances.

It should surprise no one if the peoples of Europe and the United States have doubts about their profound unity; nothing is being done to convince them of it, to create a feeling common to all. There is also the fact that the policies followed by their governments are neither discussed together, nor defined together, nor applied together. Yet the realities are there. The arts, film, music, clothing, way of life, aspirations and dreams are, if not identical, then at least closely related, especially among the younger generation.

The path is laid out for them. Europe and America must awaken to the shared civilization that unites them, and must build common institutions that enable them to act together in a world where they are no longer the exclusive holders of power.

V

❧

EUROPE NEEDS TO PREVENT AMERICAN ISOLATIONISM AND WITHDRAWAL

Conformism has its conveniences as well as its dangers. We can gladly reiterate the point that American "unilateralism" must be opposed. The phenomenon is quite real; indeed, there have been cases of it that verge on caricature. But let us not forget that, for the United States, imperialism is not as old a tradition, and perhaps not as natural a tradition, as isolationism. In the future, the most likely danger is not that America will constantly intervene in all of the affairs of the world—especially since it no longer has the means for domination on all fronts—but that it will no longer feel necessarily concerned about the issues far beyond its shores that trouble the world, and will instead pull back to focus on a few objectives of vital national importance. A country concerned only with its own prosperity and security, one that imagines that it must restrict itself to defending its selfish interests and believes it has nothing to fear from anyone, may be inclined to seek protection behind a great wall: venturing out only when it sees fit, using globalization exclusively for its own ends, and letting that be the limit of its ambitions. A certain measure of idealism is necessary for those who seek to play a role in the world. Indifference to that which is outside the self is the temptation of the powerful grown weary of disappointment. Globalization only renders this temptation more natural.

It is true that September 11th brought a harsh reality home to Americans. They understood that at best they were not invulnerable to all threats, at worst they were the preferred targets of such threats; and that, while they cannot intervene constantly all over the world or provide their own solutions to all conflicts, nevertheless isolation would ward off none of the dangers, be it terrorism, nuclear proliferation, international crime, pandemics, trade wars, or financial and monetary chaos. Thus, again, one must know which dangers one is capable of doing something about and with what means. Iraq is the most painful example of the tragedy that can be caused by a misjudgment based on ignorance of the world coupled with an ideological bias. The nearly unconditional support provided to date for Israel's policies is yet another example.

The time has come for Europe to awake to a cardinal reality: America's failures and mistakes weaken rather than strengthen Europe. One need only consider the Near East and relations with Iran. The fate of the power and influence of Europe is bound up with that of America. Conversely, when these two powers act as confident partners serving a just cause, they meet with success. We witnessed this with the end of the Cold War and the downfall of communism. We see evidence of this success today in economic globalization, which represents enormous progress in comparison to the triumphant bureaucracy and protectionism of the post-1945 period.

A weak America is not in Europe's interest; quite the contrary. A strong, confident America, one that does not seek to impose its views on everyone, is the best guarantee of overall stability and security.

This does not mean that Europe must renounce its own way of seeing things in favor of that of its natural partner. But it too must make an effort to broaden its notions, abandon prefabricated ideas, and evolve. It must try to adopt positions—on global warming, on international trade, on relations with China—that are realistic and not necessarily in opposition at every point to those of the United States. It must strive to contribute to the stabilization and reconstruction of Iraq to the extent this remains possible, and to play a more active role in resolving the conflict between Israel and Palestine. China, for example, must be treated with respect, but not pandered to. While it is clearly an emerging—and troubling—economic partner, China is also becoming a military power that is disturbing the game, and a major political competitor for the entire West, not just for the United States. It is the main beneficiary of the relative weakening of America, a situation from which Europe cannot hope to gain anything. Europe too, even while conducting its own policy, must give up the illusion of being able to profit beyond a limited point from the game of separate power, and get out while the going is still good.

Europeans and Americans alike should avoid useless provocation and mistakes that affect them mutually. This can and should be done without renouncing any part of their respective independence of judgment and action. Europe gains nothing from systematic hostility toward American policy; America gains nothing from neglecting European wishes and interests. Indeed, their quarrels are raising doubts in people's minds about the solidity of the West and its faith in itself.

৵

Europe and America must work out an ambitious partnership that deals with all of the problems they share, and must create enough solidarity to remedy the state of disarray that endangers the peoples of the West.

They need to show the capacity to act on the matter of tightening their bonds and building a more dynamic and comprehensive alliance; this would in turn make for better coordination of their specific actions around the world. Europe would emerge from its apathy; the United States would resign itself to no longer seeking to impose its views on its allies. The United States would be able to temper its messianic approach and adopt a more open-minded attitude if Europe were able to express more often its own will in international organizations and gain more respect. That is not always the case. The American administration and elites must agree to reexamine their instinctive attitudes, bring them into question, and take up a more balanced and therefore more lucid vision of international life. Building a partnership with Europe based on the recognition of the proper status of each would help this to come about.

Let us not quibble over words: A multipolar world? A multilateral world? No formula guarantees stability or security. In one perspective on today's reality, one could organize peace and harmony by grouping all the countries around a few great powers that would impose their influence on the others as if upon vassals. Acceptance of the existence of a European pole, across from an American pole, a Chinese pole, an Indian pole, a Russian pole, might bring a temporary equilibrium among nations. But is this not already an outdated vision of history? In the future, the world's conflicts will not start between the largest countries, which are all too aware of their interests, but rather between the weaker nations, which could drag their allies into their own disputes. Is this not what we witnessed in 1914? Is it not what may be seen today in Asia and Africa? Who can predict what effects the situation in Kosovo, Sudan, Afghanistan or Pakistan will have on relations among the great powers and on world peace? Agreement among these powers, with each dominating a particular region, is not sufficient. Sphere of influence politics has its limitations in this era of globalization.

International life must be imagined in such a form that decisions are made, not unilaterally by one, two or three dominant powers that get along, but rather in the context of negotiations held as frequently and on as wide a scale as possible, involving all the states concerned and that would be called upon to cooperate. The institutions for such a system already exist. Europe must convince the United States that international law has to be recognized by all, including the strongest, and that all peoples must have a say in the matter. Force, furthermore, may only be used in the service of the law, and the world's fate may not be placed exclusively in the hands of the strongest, even if it is greatly dependent upon them.

At the end of the day, what would this approach mean for Americans? They would have to change their mindset and take a clearer look at the future. Is this an easy task? Of course not. Changing one's mentality is never easy. But it would not be necessary to upset the structures of American society or effect profound institutional changes to achieve this end. All that would be needed is an effort of collective analysis and reflection. After all, Spain, France, England and Germany each in its turn had to admit that none of them could lay down the law for the rest of the world.

For the Europeans, the task would be rougher. Multiple states with multiple languages divide them, the memories of their history restrict them, and they remain resolutely attached to preserving the character of their nations and their independence. Are they ready for this revolution? One wonders.

VI

৵

The European Union and a Union of the West

Europe must not be merely a reasonable counselor half-heeded on occasion, but a respected ally. The European Union must first exist if it is to make proposals, act independently, and convince the United States as well when it deems it important to give it a warning or to carry out a joint action with it. Given the diplomatic and military experience of its member states, the European Union is uniquely qualified to play this role. Furthermore, Europe is situated at the crossroads of Africa, the Middle East and Central Asia, where it is directly confronted by the tensions that undermine these regions. But Europe must acquire the means to shoulder this responsibility. It only avoids this by focusing on trifles, such as regulating the size of rear-view mirrors on trucks, an approach that does little but under-mine its popularity and make it look silly. Europe must attend to what is essential and forget what is not.

No one should deny how much is at stake. Europe must choose and agree to undertake pro-found reforms if it simply wants to exist. Paradoxically, as soon as anyone brings up this goal, two opposite groups appear in support. There are the impassioned defenders of the West who want to make Europe the unconditional ally of the United States. On the other side are those who want to build up Europe so as to shake off American domination.

Yet another group considers reforms useless, because in its view Europe itself is useless and only the member states count. We are familiar with this argument. Under De Gaulle, France ac-quired a deterrent force, an independent foreign policy, and the power to decide things for itself. It has ideas on the future of Europe, how to orga-nize the world, the economy, global warming, and human rights. To be sure, France must be-ware of pompous unrealistic sermons, relying on the force of words, or "human-rightsism"; never-theless, as a nation France matters. We are ad-vised to think twice about adopting the basic premise according to which nation states are outdated, archaic and responsible for the ills of the world, which justifies their replacement by a superstructure that would render the nation state even more obsolete. Would Europeans want to live in a post-national world where they are no longer protected by anything more than Europe itself? It is said we are deluding ourselves. Neither a stronger Europe nor a more efficient international system can be built with weakened states. The world needs strong states, the only possible foundation of a world order.

And let us not think, we are furthermore advised, that we can only play a role through Europe. There are many parts of the world where France's influence is sought out and French foreign policy action desired. The European Union will be stronger if it unites countries that are sure of themselves, of their legitimacy, of their future, and know what they want. The future lies in the enlargement of Europe, accompanied by reinforced cooperation among small groups of states in a "variable geometry," each differently structured according to its field of competence. In short, a "Europe of circles."

There is some truth in all of this. For a long time to come, nation states will remain useful, satisfy the longings of their citizens, enjoy an irreplaceable legitimacy, and constitute a strong presence. All of these are reasons for rebuilding the European Union on new foundations that are not rooted in pipe dreams. I appreciate the praise for the "Europe of circles"; how could I not, as I proposed it some fifteen years ago? This concept represents the only realistic way for Europe to progress even while failing to define a truly common political will.

It's useless to feed the fantasy of a federal Europe. How could a federation be possible among states separated by profound differences on policy toward the United States, or on the attitude to take toward Russia, or on the very principle of a "European power," a concept rejected by those who fear that it might lead to a break with the Americans? Who still believes in this construct? Who are its proponents? Skipping all the legal subtleties about the sources of authority, federalism may be defined in simple terms: in such a system, a state may be compelled to do what it does not want to do, or not to do what it wants to do, if a majority of other member states in the federation so dictate. Which of the larger states in Europe is willing to have imposed upon it a foreign or military policy that it does not want, to wage a war in Iraq, Afghanistan, or Darfur, or not do so, according to the wishes of the majority of its partners? None. Case closed.

What, then, about the status quo? But how can anyone expect that the European Union, with its current structure and twenty-seven members, can acquire dynamism? It could do so only after remedying the flaws that keep it ineffective. The representation of the states does not take sufficient account of population; the smaller states are overrepresented in all forums—Council, Parliament, and Commission. This is an unjust distortion and gives rise to an artificial view of reality. It detracts from the credibility and authority of any decisions made, when decisions can be made at all. The vast scope of the unanimity rule makes it impossible to express a common will on important matters. Yet, for the most part, this rule will need to be maintained as long as the inequitable representation of the states persists. Multiple languages prevent quick decisions, and often prevent the very understanding of the problems at hand. The use of only two or three languages would make it possible to work with greater clarity and alacrity. Confusion exists as to the distribution of powers between the nations and the European Union. The rules and procedures are complicated. It is sometimes said that Turkey should not join the European Union, in part because its presence would make a political Europe impossible. But with or without Turkey, the Europe of Twenty-seven is doomed to political non-existence. The Union has come to be stretched so thin, enlargement after enlargement—despite the reservations expressed at the time, not least by myself—that the rules originally conceived for the six Western European states, for the most part unchanged, are inoperative.

If we truly want to progress, the status quo is untenable. European leaders recognized this in June 2007. Following the defeat of the draft European Constitution, they extracted from the draft a few new institutional rules that would enable a European will to exist and manifest itself more clearly in the eyes of the world. Thus, the Union president's term would be lengthened (two and a half years, and renewable, instead of six months), a Foreign Affairs department organized, and somewhat more of the decisions made by a qualified majority* instead of unanimously.

---

*The EU treaties specify which matters can be decided by Qualified Majority vote, and the size of the majority, usually approximately 2/3, that constitutes a Qualified Majority in these cases. [translator's note]

This simplified treaty would save what can be saved. It is good, but it is not enough. To impart a true political existence to Europe, we have to go farther.

ↄ

Whether we speak of a Europe of states or a Europe of circles, a federal Europe or a Europe of variable geometry, these are merely instruments and formulas. There remains the matter of the goal. Are we determined to allow the emergence of a European will? No agreement has been reached on this point, yet it lies at the heart of the matter. Whatever the European states may boast in the way of ancient traditions, historic prestige, and power—material, military or economic—none carries the same weight as Russia, the United States and China do today or as India and Brazil will tomorrow. Who can dispute the need for a Europe that really exists—if its component nations want to matter—no longer alone, to be sure, but in association?

As long as Europe remains unreformed, no reform of the Atlantic Alliance will be possible. Who is unaware of the flaws of NATO? The equality of states in it is an illusion. They do not all carry the same weight, far from it. Indeed, taken as a whole, the will of all the others combined matters less than that of the United States, since England, the Netherlands and the former communist countries are more willing to align with Washington than with anybody else. How can anyone be surprised by the consequences of this state of affairs for the organization of the Alliance forces and the missions assigned to it?

There is no point in discussing a different division of responsibilities in the chains of command among participating nations, in deploring the fact that too many European states prefer to acquire their military equipment from American rather than European companies (this is nothing new!), or in regretting that the Americans, when they deem it useful, act alone in one or another region of the world, using the Alliance's collective instruments, sometimes without consulting it. This inequitable situation often leads to ineffectiveness and nourishes a sense of irresponsibility in too many European countries. As long as the United States won't agree to speak to the European Union on a one-to-one basis as equals, this problem will persist. For America to agree to treat the European Union as an equal, the Union must truly exist, it must be better organized and more mobilized, and its members must invest the necessary amount in defense. In sum, Europe must behave more responsibly. If we consider just the Near East, we can see that the passivity exhibited there by the European Union has done nothing to strengthen its prestige. For more than half a century now, the European states, with a few exceptions, the most notable of which is France, have abandoned themselves to the will of others.

༄

In its current form, the European Union is bound to disappoint. It can be made to function better—and the simplified treaty tends in that direction—but this minimal reform will not remedy its fundamental flaws. There simply cannot be true effectiveness in a Europe founded on a contrived and artificial equality among states, on the uniformity of the law governing them, and, when a question of vital importance to all is at stake, on the inability to decide with a qualified majority, due to the unjust distortion in the weighting of the votes of the states. For Europe to play an active role in political and military matters would require a surrender of sovereignty to a Union of twenty-seven countries of widely varying sizes and levels of power, with heterogeneous interests, sometimes contradictory ambitions, and traditionally hostile feelings toward one another, and that have not yet agreed upon credible and efficient procedures and decision-making rules. That such a surrender of sovereignty should occur under current circumstances is inconceivable.

Things being as they are, there is little chance—short of a revolution of minds and wills—that Europe will become anything more than a large market: a customs union and a few common economic policies. Some states, basically in the west of Europe, would decide to go farther in cooperation among themselves in order to carry more weight in military and diplomatic affairs. Let us face the fact: the European construct as it has been pursued for half a century must be reexamined. Something else needs to be imagined. This is what I called the "Europe of circles."

The Europe of circles arose from the failure of a political revolution that would have required that all nations submit to the power of a true European state, one authorized to make major decisions. Since this has not occurred, the beaten paths and ready-made designs have to be abandoned. What I proposed was at the time subjected to much criticism, claiming that this new two-tiered Europe would lead to a harmful inequality among the states. But is this not what has existed from the beginning, although we never had the courage to recognize it clearly? Europe has never been capable of progressing uniformly. Its uneven progress continues to be evident today, in the fact that not all members are associated in the common policies in the monetary, military and security spheres. Under the "circles" policy, the European Union divides itself into various categories of states, this being the only way to advance and allow the most ambitious, basically those in the west, to lead the way. I am simply asking that we acknowledge the facts.

No more ambitious project is foreseeable for the next ten years. This approach is the only way for the Europe of Twenty-Seven to have more efficient institutions and play a significant role, thanks to specialized cooperation arrangements where some states can take the lead. With such a policy, Europe could grow politically and economically stronger, and stop looking for ways to blame its shortcomings on scapegoats such as globalization, liberalism, the United States, Islamism or the European Central Bank. We would have only ourselves to answer to for our difficulties or our reluctance to reform.

This new architecture, one of concentric circles, despite casting doubt on many ideas accepted and repeated now for fifty years—such as ensuring the requisite unity by uniformity alone, or equality among all states no matter what their size—is the only path for moving forward and meeting the need for cooperation that globalization renders more urgent every day. Founded on the ideas of flexibility and a progressive dynamic, the new architecture could represent a stage or an end in itself; that would depend on what Europeans decide in the future.

❧

• The first circle—of shared codified law, a large marketplace where all would meet—would correspond to the entire European Union, initially encompassing twenty-seven states, more in the future since its attributes would not preclude further enlargement. In this unified economic space, the common ground of the Union, the elimination of customs barriers and the harmonization of legal, tax and social regulations—all monitored by the judges—would allow for growth on the basis of free competition. Members would commit, as they do today, to respecting common values regarding the rule of law, democracy, and the system of social solidarity, and to implementing common policies where each would be convinced of the advantages of collective effort, in areas such as research, transportation, the environment, and agriculture.

This circle of shared codified law, as reformed by the simplified treaty, would provide the stable presidency of the Union. The president would represent the European Union throughout the world, particularly in dealings with the United States, and would be responsible for managing the competences delegated by the member states. A true Foreign Affairs department would be created, the work of the Council of Ministers rendered more transparent, and national parliaments would be more effectively involved in the formulation of legal regulations. The economic cooperation of euro-zone members would be organized, giving the European Central Bank an equal partner in the task of coordinating them, so it would not be pilloried unjustly as if it were solely responsible for the insufficiency of economic cooperation among the states. None of the provisions of the simplified draft treaty would be called into question by this Europe of circles.

At a later stage, a debate could be opened on the respective roles of the states in the institutions, so that their actual weight and financial contribution could be taken better into account. The most populous countries would be granted a status more in keeping with their size, whether in the Commission, the Parliament or the Council of Ministers. This is the only approach that would induce these countries to accept the extension of the rule of decision by a qualified majority, the only path to progress in sectors as essential as taxation or social issues. Everything is linked.

Relations between the Union's Council and Commission would be reexamined. To dispel any confusion, the Commission would be made available to the European Council, which, thanks to a more stable presidential term, would enjoy greater authority and become the veritable driving force behind collective action. Instituting a Union president who remains in office for two and a half or even five years is not without consequence for the hierarchy of powers. Experience will show that the simplified treaty does not represent a minor modification to the current architecture.

Without such a reform, the European Union,

paralyzed by the ever growing number of its members, the divergence of their interests, and the heaviness of its decision-making procedures, will soon be no more than a vast commercial market. While certainly useful, since it would still permit a free circulation of persons and goods, it would be insufficient, threatened with dilution, and ever less able to pursue common policies.

• Inside this first circle, a second one—the circle of specialized cooperation bodies—would take shape. It would bring together the more ambitious states, determined to move faster and farther together. Indeed, this circle already exists. However, it is regarded with suspicion, treated as an exception and as doomed to disappear, since it stands contrary to uniformity, the alleged guarantor of equal respect for the prerogatives of each state. Let us see things as they are: diversity is the only way for Europe to progress and avoid paralysis and dissension.

The task of closer cooperation must be made easier for those member states that are so inclined in particular spheres. They could organize together without having to go through community procedures—the Commission, the Parliament, the Council of Ministers. These cooperation arrangements would bring together different states according to the function involved. The idea would not be to constitute a sort of "core" of the Union that always includes the same states, those always ahead of the others, but rather to enable the willing to act together on matters of security, defense, diplomacy, currency, the environment, or research, to name just a few areas. These associations would allow their members extensive delegations of sovereignty. They would not be closed; their vocation would be to expand so as to include all the members of the Union. They would simply take the lead and set an example. Voluntary service would not detract from unity.

• The third circle would be external to the Union. It would encompass neighboring states with which the Union would conclude close partnership agreements. These agreements, which are mainly economic and commercial, should all have a common base of political commitments: respect for the rights of minorities and existing borders, and adherence to the principles of democracy; that was how it was done in the stability pact I initiated in 1993 to make it possible to include the former satellites of the Soviet Union in an enlarged Europe.

For those states that seek close ties with the Union but are not ready or inclined to fulfill all of the conditions for membership, or do not share an unequivocal European vocation, these partnerships would provide the Union a way to link them to itself. For some countries, these partnerships would constitute a final goal, for others a necessary stage before their full integration into the Union as regular members. The countries of the southern and eastern Mediterranean would be candidates for such partnerships.

꒳

Reconstructed in this way, the Union would be able to express a stronger will and set greater ambitions for itself. When the whole group is unable to act, certain states could fill in until such time as the entire Union is ready to take over the task. It would be incumbent upon the "Europe of circles" to establish two priority objectives: research and education, necessary conditions for economic progress and therefore for the Union's capacity for action; and diplomacy and defense, to be achieved through a much closer military cooperation among France, Germany, Great Britain, Italy and Spain, thereby enabling easier resolution of such matters as the construction of a European aircraft carrier, the fight against terrorism, or the pooling of military industries.

And so the goal would be achieved: Europe would become a partner of equal importance to the United States, one that is strong, reliable, respected, and just as cohesive, and without whose agreement no joint action would be conceivable. Failing this, the Union of the West will not see the light of day.

VII

꒕

Specific Steps toward a Union of the West

The European Union, once reorganized, could bring about a closer cooperation* with the United States. This would provide greater security and broader influence for both.

• Proposals for this, already made at my initiative a few years ago, include: the appointment of a European coordinator of transatlantic relations working directly under the European Union president; and the creation by the Euro-

---

*In the European Union, "a cooperation" has a technical meaning, building on the ordinary meaning of the word. It refers to an arrangement for cooperation among a group of countries, specifying matters to be dealt with together and often procedures and structures for doing so. It is distinct from "a common action," which refers to an action to be taken together by the member states through EU standard procedures and institutions. [translator's note]

pean Union and the United States of a permanent joint secretariat, tasked with preparing meetings between ministers or heads of state, meetings of the multilateral financial institutions they take part in, and negotiations conducted within the World Trade Organization. The purpose would be to avoid coming out with divergent positions in international forums and to examine measures for deepening economic integration on both sides of the Atlantic.

• Other essential issues could be discussed to harmonize the American and European points of view. These would include the acquisition of nuclear weapons by internally fragile states of questionable democratic principles. Such acquisitions constitute a risk that is further magnified by the fact that they make the Non-Proliferation Treaty even more vulnerable. Additionally, a better division of the financial burdens of military spending could be discussed in order to achieve a more balanced approach, with Europe taking on a more equitable share, more in line with its financial means and security needs. As a result of this, a decision could finally be made on a more equitable distribution of commands and responsibilities within the Alliance.

• These are fine intentions, and they lay the

ground for concrete measures, but they are still too timid. Europe and the United States should show greater ambition and conceive of the gradual creation of a large common market, with the institution of a customs union and the adoption of similar regulations for fiscal and juridical matters and competition law. An immense arena, stretching across the Atlantic, would in this way be opened up for the formation of an economic and social community governed as far as possible by the same principles and subject to the same rules. Who can fail to see that under such circumstances discussions at the International Monetary Fund, the World Trade Organization or the G8 would unfold under better conditions for interests that, little by little, would become if not common then at least infinitely closer?

- It is time to seriously commit to putting an end to the disorderly floating of currencies that threatens the prosperity and progress of the world and that will eventually destroy the very idea of economic liberalism. In 1986, I was able to get our partners to sign the Louvre Accords, in which Europe, the United States and Japan pledged to maintain monetary stability through coordination of their economic policies and interventions by the central banks on the foreign exchange market. For a few years the Accords yielded satis-factory results, before they were forgotten and monetary speculation resumed with renewed vigor.

Subsequently I attempted on several occasions to convince France's partners to take up a more stable international monetary system. I did not succeed. All refused the modicum of discipline needed to prevent currency values from fluctuat-ing excessively and to keep them in tune with economic realities. Their refusal was in the name of a false and unbridled concept of liberty. Liberty is not synonymous with letting things go their own way; on the contrary, it presupposes that common principles are defined and respected. Today we can see where this myopia is leading us: anarchic capital flows, monetary instability, uncontrolled underwriting of credit with no con-nection to the real needs of the economy, and apologetics for extremely short-term profiteering that lacks any justification. These factors in turn engender chaos, anxiety, and crisis, with no com-mon authority in a position to impose a few in-dispensable rules backed by just sanctions.

We must not lose heart, but take up the task again. Thanks to the felicitous creation of the euro, the franc and the mark no longer fluctuate in relation to one another and commercial transactions within the Union are safe from speculation. Today the ratios that matter are those between the euro and the dollar. We cannot suggest the creation of a currency common to Europe and America; considering the global role of the dollar, it would be too unequal a marriage. On the other hand, a relationship akin to that instituted among European currencies by the European Monetary System could be imagined between the dollar and the euro, with the fluctuation margins guided and controlled by the two central banks, the Fed and the European Central Bank, the economic and budgetary policies coordinated, and the monetary policies harmonized. Is this too great an ambition? I am convinced of the opposite: I strongly believe that liberalism is advantageous only when accompanied by an order, that is, a set of rules that must be respected by all. The world will know neither balance nor lasting prosperity as long as monetary stability is not guaranteed. Today it is not; worse, the currency fluctuations are rationalized by the argument that only a freely functioning market can bring stable and lasting prosperity. It is time to let go of these prefabricated ideas.

• In the realm of foreign policy, this new

Union between Europe and the United States would require that each pledge not to take any important initiative without first having conferred with the other. This would avert such controversies and misunderstandings as those that arose from America's intention to install an anti-missile shield in Eastern Europe. Looking farther ahead, both partners would define new objectives in their relations with the rest of the world, such as a heightened concern for human rights, a declared intention to protect the environment, and credible action to assist in the development of poorer countries.

• As regards military issues, the emergence of a Union of the West between Europe and the United States would make it possible to rebalance the functioning of the Alliance for a better distribution of responsibilities, since American reticence would no longer be justified. The Alliance would no longer evade the need to update and clarify the strategic concept that underlies it, defining for today's world the defense mission that had once justified its creation, the conditions for it to intervene outside of its traditional geographical area (which is itself expanding), and the rules allowing its members to intervene in one or another region of the world without the consent of their allies while nonetheless using the instruments of the Alliance.

Such adjustments become all the more necessary as the United States and Europe must act in concert—in Africa, for example, to keep the continent from sinking into poverty, overpopulation, tribal wars and tyrannies; or in the Middle East, where much of the West's prosperity, security and even its fate are at stake.

No matter what the issue—be it energy supplies, the environment, or the fight against terrorism—the solidarity of Europe and the United States must be indivisible if they want to make the best use of the assets still at their disposal thanks to their current strength and the political influence they still possess. This would seem undeniable.

ༀ

The most serious problem faced by Europe and America is the nuclear issue in all its facets. It is critical that these two powers harmonize their thinking and synchronize their policies in this area. They must avoid creating tensions and exposing themselves to risks of reprisals by undertaking abrupt and poorly understood initiatives. The creation by the Americans of an antimissile shield in Eastern Europe is a case in point. Even if the Alliance in the end resigned itself to the American action, it was not done without difficulty, and the matter will have lasting effects. Moreover, it is not really settled.

- France, for its part, will need to reconsider the conditions under which it would use the nuclear weapons that it acquired with good reason half a century ago. These conditions are no longer the same.

Does the concept of deterrence of the strong by the weak have the same meaning as before, given the growing destructive capabilities of weapons and the medium size of a country such as France? A few strikes could destroy it completely, causing its population, its culture, its landscape, even life itself to disappear, and wipe it off the face of the earth. Other, much larger countries, such as China, Russia, or the United States, given their surface areas, could undergo an equivalent level of destruction without ever being annihilated or disappearing from the scene. Is deterrence of the strong by the weak credible if the weak are so vulnerable and run risks so much greater in the event of a reprisal, when the countries pitted against each other would be of such different dimensions and not subject to the same dangers? Here we are reduced to conjecture. Would the greatest risk incurred by countries of medium size necessarily dissuade them from using nuclear weapons in an act of desperation? Who could say for sure that when Hitler was holed up in a Berlin in ruins in April 1945 he would not have resorted to use of nuclear weapons if they had been available to him?

As a result, we could be tempted to rethink the traditional doctrine of using the least powerful tactical nuclear weapons as a final warning before resorting to strategic nuclear weapons, and only in that case. Since the effects of these weapons are less formidable, they would be used as a weapon on the field of battle. Their use would be trivialized, the distinction between conventional and nuclear weapons blurred on the level of their use. All the points of reference of military thinking would be disrupted. Here some fresh thinking, free of traditional prejudice, is needed. Nothing is to be gained by obscuring these problems or by endlessly rehashing the same old logic.

• There is more: Europe will not truly exist until the day it can ensure its own security and is protected against nuclear attack, not only by the United States but by its own means. Only France can offer this guarantee to Europe, as the British forces are not sufficiently autonomous from the United States. Is France prepared to put its force at the disposition of a European power that would need to be a federal power, with immediate decision-making competence in the hands of a single responsible official? It would be pointless even to dream of such a thing for several decades to come. Is France ready to commit to protecting all of the members of the Union, offering them the guarantee of recourse to its nuclear weapons if needed? This would be a huge decision, carrying immense dangers for France if it were to be dragged into conflicts it had nothing to do with, far from its shores, and beyond its control. The most plausible scenario, perhaps the most desirable one, is that for now things remain as they are, and that France stick to respecting the principle of the sovereignty of states, beginning with its own. This does not preclude thinking about the future. No nuclear state can afford to forego such reflection.

• Consideration must also be given to a problem so difficult that no one seems to want to face it directly: the future of the nuclear Non-Proliferation Treaty. Will the dissemination of scientific and technical knowledge allow the treaty to remain effective for long?

Is nuclear proliferation inevitable? Technical progress is shortening the time needed for moving from civil to military nuclear technology. The international community is finding it hard to apply lasting and effective sanctions on those countries that want access to this technology; countries that, for demographic, geographic and economic reasons, enjoy the political and moral support of hundreds of millions of people. The Non-Proliferation Treaty has already been violated on numerous occasions by certain signatory states. Others that have not signed on to it free themselves of its restrictions with the tacit acquiescence of the international community. Under such circumstances this treaty is at risk of becoming obsolete. What approach can be taken to address this new situation in which threats, pressures and sanctions prove of doubtful effectiveness? What can be done when the great powers appear not to show the same severity toward all states that fail to implement the treaty, and in the end simply acknowledge this fact, as the United States did with India? Who will judge the gravity of the danger presented by one or the other? How can we respond to a nuclear proliferation that is spreading not only to states but also to criminal organizations? The latter benefit from greater access to the knowledge and techniques disseminated by states that are at odds with the international community.

To ward off this danger, planning is already underway for the construction of antimissile shields that, in order to be effective, must be installed with the agreement of several countries and aimed in every direction. From the West's point of view, the scale for the conception and use of such shields cannot be anything short of the entire space of the Atlantic Alliance. Can we go even further and propose a general renunciation of nuclear weapons? Such a proposal would destabilize relations among the armed forces of the world; it would be unacceptable to those who already have nuclear weapons, while criminal organizations would relinquish nothing. Should consideration be given to the establishment of binding international rules that would aim to lock in the present situation, with compliance enforced upon a simple report by the United Nations Security Council that they have been violated? Many states would be hostile to this basic innovation in international law and see it as legitimizing an unfair situation that favors a few, and instituting an international executive authority to consolidate it. Yet, without such a change, we will have more and more difficulty containing nuclear proliferation.

༈

To face up to such serious issues and try to find answers, an organized and improved cooperation between Europeans and Americans is not enough, nor a deepened military Alliance either. Things must be stated clearly and for all to hear. A vaster ambition requires a new organization. We must show ourselves to be bolder and build—these words have a meaning—a true Union of the West traversing the two shores of the ocean. France is part of the European Union; it is committed to the creation of a Mediterranean Union; the interests of Europe go farther. The Union of the West would complete the construction of a new system of progress and security. This would benefit both Europeans and Americans.

The Union of the West would have an Executive Council, convening its leaders every three months. Which leaders would they be? For the United States it would be simple: the president, aided by the cabinet secretaries of his choice. For the European Union things are less clear: the president of the Union, certainly, for general matters, acting on the mandate of the European Council and aided by authoritative personages it would designate. But when matters that do not concern all members of the Union, such as currency or defense, are to be discussed, one could imagine the European Union being represented by its president and assisted by the president of the group of states united for the specialized co-operation, such as the president of the euro group for monetary matters. It would be best to retain an ability to adapt as experience dictates and avoid getting locked up in rigid formulas.

Would this Executive Council have as its sole mission to organize the debate, harmonize the positions of its members and—this would be the new factor—to do so at regular intervals? Should it be endowed, like the European Council, with true decision-making authority? If so, in what form and with what majority and sanctions? It is too early to answer such questions without running the risk of daydreaming. It would already be enormous progress if a body were to be created on an initially limited basis and were to meet frequently, and if neither the Europeans nor the Americans could decide anything on matters of common interest without having discussed them together beforehand. If this endeavor had positive results, then the Union of the West could go farther. But to be frank, I do not see this as a possibility today.

The goal of organizing a coherent and effective Atlantic community will remain a dream if Europeans and Americans, who have a common interest in putting an end to their quarrels, do not give themselves the legal instruments to do so by creating a Union of the West. This Union would need sound institutions. That is the task of the next generation.

VIII

৵

DOES THE WEST HAVE ANY OTHER CHOICE?

No one is capable of defining a different choice that is realistic. Many however, object to the very principle of a closer association between Europe and the United States in the name of protecting an ever more fragile independence. They fail to see that to refuse this association would mean clouding the future for both.

The aim proposed is immense. It will be no easy task for each to accept that an era of history has come to an end, and to renounce exercising alone the powers that it can no longer handle effectively, so as to benefit from a strength that will be greater though collective. If the creation of the Union of Europe is presented as an undertaking without precedent, then the Union of the West itself, spanning the Atlantic, will be worthy of no less praise.

It is the grand design of the half-century to come. The time has come to make it a reality. Its achievement will give rise to countless difficulties, the greatest from the Western nations themselves, where past rivalries, conformism and lack of imagination continue to inform their policies. But there is no alternative and nobody has proposed one, other than the status quo from which a slow and continuous weakening will result, then decadence, as new powers emerge around the world.

To achieve a better balance, this Union of the West assumes that the partners are of comparable strength on either side of the Atlantic. A revolution of mindset is needed, both in Europe and the United States. Each must stop harboring nostalgic and inconsistent ways of thinking.

Europeans want to keep their distance from the United States, dreading too close an association out of fear of being kept under a prolonged trusteeship. Yet they lack the resolution to truly unite themselves, the only way they can level the playing field with the United States and have nothing more to fear for their independence.

As for the Americans, they would be glad to preserve the status quo. To be sure, the United States knows that the period of its exclusive worldwide domination, following the collapse of the Soviet Union, has passed, and the world has entered into another epoch of power relations. As Brent Scowcroft writes, its ships, aircraft, armored vehicles, satellites and missiles are of little use against terrorist organizations. But Americans continue to believe that very little can be accomplished without their leadership, so their leadership is still indispensable. This is true today, but won't be for long. Within twenty years, many are the changes that will occur in the balance of power!

Time is of the essence for both. The United States must convince itself that it will be more successful in maintaining the world's equilibrium if it is more closely connected to a Europe that is at long last organized. It will have to make a break with its habit of deciding things alone, which is explained if not justified by the role it played in defending liberty throughout the twentieth century. The United States needs to recognize that isolation weakens it too, as the adventure in Iraq shows, and the time has passed for military solutions that no one approves. Asia's rise in power will force it to make compromises. America will be more powerful if it is no longer alone, but strongly linked to others, even at some expense to its freedom of movement. As for the European nations, they must, without forsaking any part of themselves, open their eyes and establish closer links with one another, as this is the only way to speak to the United States on an equal basis. Europeans have to make a two-fold effort: organize a true Union among themselves and forge close ties between this new Union and the United States.

༄

There is no risk of reviving the "clash of civilizations" through Union. Nor would the decline of the West fuel it; quite the opposite. A peaceful dialogue between civilizations assumes that they are speaking on an equal, one-to-one basis, that they understand each other better, that they are aware of their common interests, and that, beyond these differences that each wants to preserve, they respect one another's principles and originality. Once the West is organized, that is to say, re-equilibrated, and more aware of its limits, less imbued with its superiority, having given up on imposing its domination as a remedy to a sense of vulnerability that it has to live with, it will then be seen in a different light by the peoples of the world.

The world truly needs to be taken as it is, in all its diversity and vitality, and the extraordinary will to progress that from now on animates the main part of humanity, too long consigned to the margins of history. In these new times, other civilizations are emerging, but the West continues to exist; it too is a reality, a constituent part of humanity, for a long time the most enlightened and dynamic. To declare that the West exists, to want it to survive in a world where it will represent less wealth and power in relation to others, implies that Europeans and Americans should not dissipate their energies in the many contradictions of the past, or indulge in rivalries that no longer make sense; that, instead of cultivating their mutual resentments, they should rather focus on what they have in common.

Will the strength of national sentiment stand in the way of such a trend? As time passes, we are able to look beyond antiquated arguments and see the truth. For Europe, it is not about creating a superstate that denies the permanence of nations. The European Union will continue to be enriched by the cultural diversity of the countries that constitute it, by their languages, their traditions, and their moral, religious and artistic sensibilities. Each nation will retain its uniqueness and have the means to better preserve it. Only the weak and the timid are obsessed with the risk of uniformity. Globalization is developing relationships and increasing the similarities among lifestyles and even modes of thought among the peoples of the world, but it is doing so without touching what is essential: their soul. The Chinese are not likely to resemble the Americans, or the French to resemble the Japanese!

Another oft-raised objection is that the United States and Europe do not have the same interests, the same ambitions, the same views, or the same policies toward all peoples, and should therefore not be locked into a dialogue that excludes all others. Certainly, but should this be allowed to undermine their will to engage in joint action? Europe would not be led by the United States to adopt a policy toward China, Japan, Taiwan, North Korea or Central Asia that is contrary to its wishes. Europe's positions are sometimes different from America's. To try to harmonize these positions, to be bound to make every effort to do so, would not cause Europe to become soft or to promote interests that are contrary to its own. Would the European Union refrain from proceeding with independent action in Africa, the Near East or Eastern Europe, if it were to one day become capable of such action, or subordinate its positions to those of the United States? Hardly. Would Europe neglect Russia's reinvigorated presence and strength on the continent, which require it to take certain precautions to the extent allowed by its moral principles? No.

Each of the two partners has its own commitments that it intends to keep. Both will belong to several organizations: For America, there is the Union of the West, the Atlantic Alliance, the security and assistance pacts that link it to several Asian nations, the North American Free Trade Agreement that it intends to extend to the southern part of the hemisphere. For Europe, the Union of the West again, the European Union, the Mediterranean Union if it sees the light of day, not to mention the close partnerships that it will establish with Russia, centuries-old ally of France, and with Turkey, Africa and others. Each will have to prioritize its choices and make them compatible with one another. Will the task be any more difficult than it is today, when improvisation and disorganization lead to misunderstandings and chaos and cause great damage? Will this multiplicity of memberships in various organizations prove too complicated for the United States or for the European Union to manage? But is the current situation, with its labyrinth of organizations and resulting chaos, any simpler or more efficient? Certainly not.

The closer association between Europe and the

United States would not always lead them to identical policies in all regions of the world, but at the very least they would hold discussions beforehand and better understand one another, perhaps even reach agreement. Europe is not focused exclusively on the Atlantic, but also on Africa and Eastern Europe, and on Russia in particular. The United States is concerned not only with events in Europe, but also with those in Latin America and in the Pacific, an area that is looming ever larger in its fears and apprehensions. This multiplicity of interests does not constitute an obstacle to bringing Europe and America together. Quite the contrary: each, thanks to the other, would have a more sound view of the state of the world and the most appropriate actions to be undertaken. Many ambiguities would be dissipated, misunderstandings clarified, rivalries avoided.

တ

For the West, organizing itself better would not mean closing itself off with a purely defensive attitude. The West's mission is not to reject the world but, on the contrary, to send it a message of solidarity and cooperation. It is to call upon the international community to awaken to the risks of violence and chaos flowing from terrorism, climate change, nuclear proliferation, and poverty—risks that threaten all peoples, whatever their religion, culture, race or history—and to act together to confront them.

Thus would the West revive its age-old mission that the tragedies of the twentieth century have obscured: To present a common concept to the world that will unite it, a universalism that is free of uniformity and respects the personality of each, instead of conflicts between hostile civilizations. The finest part of the Western heritage is its vision of a mankind in which the equal dignity of all is recognized and in which respect is assured for the freedom of men and of nations, and for their diversity. It is a sort of idealism, that tolerance and reason reign, not murderous passions. The West must tirelessly lead by example and show firmness in defending democratic values.

Only then will the West rediscover a role measuring up to the one it played for four centuries, when it disseminated, through intellectual reforms and an economic revolution, a material civilization that no longer has any rival, and tried to spread the acceptance of principles of collective life founded on freedom; but when it also subjected peoples to a political domination that it considered justified on the basis of its preeminence. Today the West must endure the consequences of this contradiction, and the hostility that it aroused. It now has to show that its messianism was more than just hypocrisy. The world needs a spiritual message, one that goes beyond its differences and confrontations. If the West demonstrates its ability to be tolerant, selfless, idealistic and intelligent, it can rediscover a mission commensurate with its history without sacrificing any part of its material influence. But it must convince others of its sincerity. Concrete actions will be needed.

Will the West reach the goal? It will, if Europe, after the two civil wars that tore it apart and brought it to its knees in the course of the twentieth century, agrees to end its infighting and build its peace, influence and prosperity, adopting the institutions that would make this possible, and so truly exist; and if the United States for its part agrees no longer to try to decide everything alone as it has so often done, and recognizes that there are alternatives to the isolationism and imperialism between which it has always swung. Then it would become possible to forge a true Union of the West. For all involved, it would be the sort of revolution that creates a future. Is this too grand an ambition? No other can enable the West to escape the decline that threatens it. Given the new powers that are emerging, only Union will enable the West to assert itself in the century that is now beginning.

Most importantly, the West must set for itself the goal of presenting to the world a message that is above all moral and political, founded on universal endorsement of common values and universal respect for them. This is not a fanciful mission; it alone will allow the West to regain the image it once claimed as its own in the eyes of the world. In a sense the West would be returning to its roots, but to roots that have been purged of the burdens of the ashes of history.

༄

It is up to France to seize the initiative on this Union of the West for its European partners and the Americans. France need not fear that in so doing it will see its role shrunk to the European space. Just the opposite. It will retain an active and useful role in Francophone countries, like Great Britain in the Commonwealth. It will have an economic, financial and commercial power all its own, if it can reform. Its traditions and status will ensure that it preserves its influence in the Near East and Africa. And in line with the mission it has given itself, it will remain one of the defenders of the great moral principles that preserve the peace among the nations and the equilibrium of the world.

Would the Union of the West lead France to be subjugated to American positions? The time has come to stop cultivating these fantasies, which are anti-European as well as anti-American. They are kept alive in the name of a false idea of nation. The stronger Europe is, the stronger France will be. The stronger Europe is, the better it will be able to avoid the "clash of civilizations" and, thanks to an improved association with America, to influence the latter to work for peace. Are we sure that the moment might not soon arrive in which Americans themselves come to this realization?

To be credible, to at the very least have its proposals examined, France must break with a pseudo-lyrical and truly exaggerated arrogance that, as experience has shown, has not brought it any success. France must also leave behind a systematically anti-American attitude that has isolated it and deprived it of all credibility with its partners; something it can do without bending to anyone's injunctions or copying their decisions. Finally, France must accept Europe's becoming a true political actor, with its own will and means adequate to the task.

Instead of thinking of Europe, in which France long played a leading role, as chipping away at its own power, France should have an ambition for Europe itself. Let it take bold initiatives, as it did a half-century ago when it proposed the creation of the Community. It took a lot of temerity and imagination back then to envisage a reconciliation between France and Germany. These qualities are needed today to break away from the psychological reflexes and habits that paralyze the spirit, and propose a new policy to Europe and America. In so doing, France will not court any danger. It will not—not France!—be suspected of favoring a war of civilizations. Rather, it will remain faithful to the noblest of the convictions that gave its history its grandeur. And it will win greater prestige.

Let us become aware that we are entering a new world! In this world, it is only by combining imagination, generosity and realism that we can safeguard our idea of man and of international society.

BY THE SAME AUTHOR

L'Arbre de mai (Atelier Marcel Jullian, 1979).

Je crois en l'homme plus qu'en l'Etat (Flammarion, 1987).

Passion et Longueur de temps (Fayard, 1989).

Douze lettres aux Français trop tranquilles (Fayard, 1990).

Des modes et des convictions (Fayard, 1992).

Dictionnaire de la réforme (Fayard, 1992).

Deux ans à Matignon (Plon, 1995).

Caractère de la France (Plon, 1997).

L'Avenir de la différence (Plon, 1999).

Renaissance de la droite (Plon, 2000).

Les Aventuriers de l'Histoire (Plon, 2001).

Jeanne d'Arc et la France, le mythe du sauveur (Fayard, 2003).

La Fin de l'illusion jacobine (Fayard, 2004).

Machiavel en démocratie (Fayard, 2006).

L'Europe autrement (Fayard, 2006).

Laissons de Gaulle en paix! (Fayard, 2006).